Reptiles

Written by Joyce Pope
Illustrated by Michael Posen

p

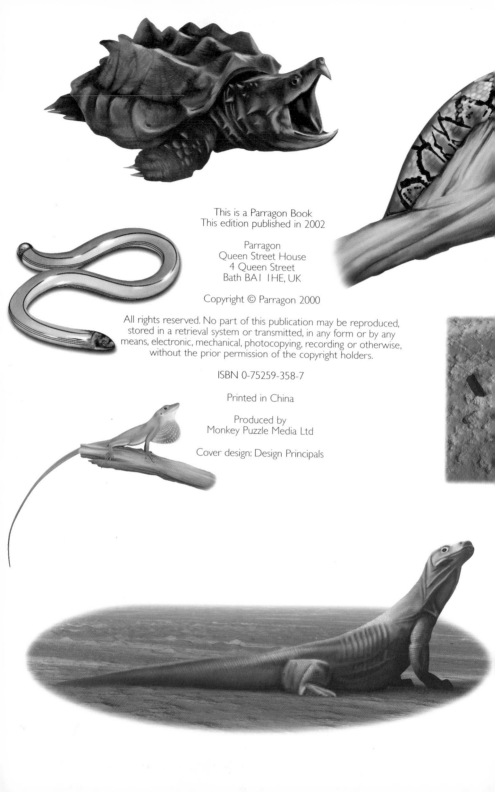

This is a Parragon Book
This edition published in 2002

Parragon
Queen Street House
4 Queen Street
Bath BA1 1HE, UK

ISBN 0-75259-358-7

Printed in China

Produced by
Monkey Puzzle Media Ltd

Cover design: Design Principals

Contents

This Nile crocodile has a typically pointed snout.   **Nile crocodile**

Do all reptiles look alike?

No! THE SLOW-MOVING TORTOISES AND THEIR RELATIVES ARE SHAPED

like half an orange, and covered in armour made of bone and horn. Crocodiles have sprawly legs and long tails, flattened at the sides. They are armoured with little plates of bone. Lizards also have sprawly legs but they have a scaly skin, which is often brightly coloured. And, of course, snakes have no legs at all.

Are reptiles terrifically noisy animals?

Most reptiles are very quiet. But some hiss with anger or fear. Some make grunts or barking calls when they are up and about at night to keep in touch with each other. Crocodiles are the noisiest reptiles – they can roar like a lion.

When are reptiles invisible?

Some reptiles are brightly coloured and easy to see. But most are camouflaged with shades of brown, green and grey, so that they disappear into their background. Often they sit very still and are almost impossible to spot.

Have some reptiles got three eyes?

Not three eyes that can focus and actually see things, but many reptiles have a light-sensitive area in the top of their head, and this is some-times called a third eye. The "third eye" may act as a short-cut to the brain and some actions that depend on light are probably controlled by it.

So, what is a reptile?

A reptile is an animal that you are most likely to see in the warmer parts of the world. It may be smaller than one of your fingers, or many times as big as you are. But like you, it will always have a skeleton and it will breathe air. It may be brightly coloured or dull shades of brown or grey, but its skin will be hard and dry to the touch.

What does cold-blooded mean?

Cold-blooded means that an animal does not have a thermostat inside its brain, like we do, to keep its body at the same temperature all the time. Cold-blooded animals like reptiles rely on the Sun to heat them up.

How many kinds of reptiles are there?

There are about 6,000 different kinds of reptiles. These can be divided into groups that include around 20 crocodiles and alligators; 600 tortoises, terrapins and turtles; 2,500 lizards, and a similar number of snakes. One group contains only one animal – a living fossil called the tuatara.

Iguanas belong to the lizard family. This one is sunning itself on a tree branch.

Green iguana

What is the world's smallest reptile?

The smallest of all reptiles are dwarf geckos, which live in the West Indies. They are less than 6 cm (2 in) long when fully grown – and over half of this length is tail! Very little is known about these tiny lizards, but like all geckos they feed on insects.

What is the world's biggest reptile?

The longest reptile is a snake called the reticulated python. It often measures over 6.1 m (18 feet). The heaviest reptile is the saltwater crocodile. An old male may weigh as much as 1,000 kg (2,200 lb).

Are reptiles very brainy beasts?

COMPARED TO MAMMALS, AND MOST OF ALL TO OURSELVES, REPTILES ARE not that smart. They use their instincts for most of the things they do. It's difficult to study the intelligence and behaviour of wild reptiles, but pet lizards can recognise their owners by voice and appearance.

Do reptiles eat a lot?

No. Cold-blooded animals live on a low-energy system. Compared to mammals they eat very little. They also breathe infrequently, except when they are very warm and active.

Reticulated python

How old do reptiles get?

As a rule, reptiles live longer than mammals or birds of a similar size. Very big reptiles live for much longer than warm-blooded animals and it's likely that a really large crocodile may have passed its 200th birthday. Big tortoises live to a similar age.

The reticulated python is happy both on land and in water.

5

Where do the biggest reptiles live?

THE LEATHERY TURTLE LIVES IN THE SEA. THE BIGGEST REPTILES OF ALL – crocodiles and the largest snakes – always live near water. Strangely, the biggest land reptiles all live on tiny islands. These include the Komodo dragon, which is the biggest lizard and lives on the island of Komodo, and the giant tortoises of the Galapagos Islands.

How do reptiles while away the winter?

Without the sun, they slow down, and some of them stop altogether! As the weather gets colder, reptiles move more slowly, eat less and rest more. In places where winter weather is really harsh, they find safe places to hibernate. Often hundreds of them sleep together through the cold season.

How do reptiles get to be on remote islands?

Scientist think that reptiles first got to small islands like Komodo by accident, probably floating on trees that were washed into the sea by big storms. Once they had reached the islands, the reptiles found that they had no enemies. They had no need to hide and in time they became very big.

When people first saw the Komodo dragon they thought it was a real dragon.

Komodo dragon

Where do reptiles live?

Reptiles make their homes in all sorts of places – in deserts and forests, on plains and in water. Sea snakes and sea turtles live in the oceans. Crocodiles are always found near water, but usually the fresh water of rivers and lakes. Many lizards and some snakes are good climbers and hunt for their prey in the branches of trees. Others burrow underground, often to escape from harsh weather. A few geckos and lizards make their homes in human houses. People often welcome them, because they eat insect pests.

Why do most reptiles live in hot places?

Because they are cold-blooded and need heating up by the sun! Reptiles use the sun's energy to keep warm, rather than making warmth for themselves, as we and other mammals do. Where the weather is hottest, life is easy for reptiles.

Which reptile lives at the North Pole?

No reptile lives right at the North Pole, but several kinds are found north of the Arctic Circle, where the weather is extremely cold for much of the year. In Europe the adder lives further north than any other reptile. You could find it in the Arctic Circle in northern Sweden and Finland.

Which reptiles like to get in the swim?

Water is the home for crocodiles and alligators, sea snakes and turtles. Terrapins live in fresh water and some snakes also spend much of their lives near rivers or lakes, though they often come on to dry land. Very few lizards are water-living creatures.

Why aren't there any snakes in Ireland?

Legend says that St Patrick cast all the snakes out of Ireland. In fact, snakes are very bad sea travellers and rarely manage to reach island homes, unlike many tortoises and lizards. At the end of the last Ice Age snakes slithered into England when it was still joined on to Europe. But by the time they reached the west coast, the sea had melted and Ireland was cut off, so the snakes were stuck in England, Wales and Scotland.

Are reptiles good at DIY?

No. Reptiles are not home-makers like many mammals. Some may dig burrows to live in, but more often they find a crack in the rocks or a hole in the ground where they can shelter. A few take advantage of the den-making skills of other creatures. The tuatara lives in a burrow made by a bird and some snakes lodge in prairie dog townships.

Sea krait

The sea krait uses its curving body to push itself through water.

Which reptiles live in trees?

FORESTS ARE THE HOME FOR MANY KINDS OF REPTILE. WITH THEIR LONG CLAWS, lizards are good climbers and even snakes squirm their way up trees to hunt birds and insects. Tortoises find shelter on the forest floor and terrapins often live in forest rivers.

How hot do reptiles like it?

Although they are cold-blooded, the body temperature of reptiles can soar to a level that would kill any mammal, so they can be happily active in heat that would be uncomfortable for us. In the hottest places it is too warm even for reptiles, so they hide underground during the daytime and come out to hunt in the cool of the night.

How do reptiles help us study evolution?

Scientists compare reptiles that are found on remote islands with their relations on the nearest mainland. They can often discover which sort of reptile reached the island first, because it has had most time to develop and so is least like its mainland cousins.

What are sidewinders?

SIDEWINDERS ARE SNAKES THAT LIVE IN SANDY DESERTS. THEY move across the loose surface by looping their bodies up in the air and pushing hard against the ground where they land. The track that a sidewinder leaves in the sand is just a series of straight lines at an angle to the direction in which it is travelling. They show where its body touched down for a moment.

Geckos are expert fly catchers.

Gecko

How speedy are reptiles?
They may look as if they are running fast, but because their bodies are generally curving from side to side, most reptiles actually move quite slowly. The fastest speed recorded for a snake is about 10 kph (6 mph) and for a lizard 27 kph (16 mph).

Can reptiles climb trees?
Many kinds of lizards live in trees, using their sharp claws to cling on as they climb. Some snakes also live in trees. They wriggle up the tree trunks, holding on with the big scales on their undersides.

Where do reptiles move faster than humans?
It's a close thing! Water reptiles such as turtles or crocodiles can outswim a human easily. On land, a really hungry crocodile could move fast enough to catch a person. Otherwise, humans can outrun most reptiles – except where the ground is very rough. Beware!

How does a snake manage without legs?
Snakes generally move by throwing their bodies into big curves and holding against the ground with the scales of their undersides. They must have a rough surface to move over. Put a snake on a piece of glass and it would wriggle about helplessly.

What runs upside-down?
Geckos are lizards that sometimes come into houses and run about on the ceiling. They do this without falling because their toes have little flaps of skin that make their feet into suction pads, which hold them safely.

8

Flying lizard

Are reptiles long-distance runners?
No. Reptiles run out of puff very quickly, so they can't run far. If a reptile has a long distance to travel it will do so slowly, in its own time.

Flying lizards glide through the air, rather than fly.

How fast does a snake strike its prey?
A striking prairie rattlesnake moves its head at an average speed of 2.44 m (8 feet) per second. But a human's fist punching towards an opponent moves faster.

How do snakes swim?
Snakes swim by curving their bodies and pushing hard against the water. Snakes that swim well are usually long and slender. Some have flattened sides, so their whole bodies are like a long paddle that moves them through the water.

Why do reptiles have a curvy walk?
Most reptiles have legs that stick out from the sides of their bodies. They always use diagonal limbs (left front foot, right hind foot) together. Because of this, they swing their bodies into a big curve, which makes it easy for them to take a long stride. Even reptiles, like snakes and some lizards that have no legs at all, move in a series of curves. Small crocodiles may gallop, but other reptiles never do, even when they are going as fast as they can. However, some lizards can run on their hind legs.

Can reptiles fly?

T HE PTEROSAURS, WHICH LIVED AT THE SAME TIME AS THE DINOSAURS, had huge bat-like wings and flew well. Today, the best that a few forest-dwelling reptiles can do is to glide from one tree to another. The champion gliders are little lizards that have long ribs, some of which they fold back against their sides.

Leaping from a branch, they spread their ribs, opening umbrella-like fans of skin. Then they glide, like brightly coloured paper darts, for up to 20 m (60 feet). Some other lizards and a few snakes flatten their bodies as they leap, but they cannot glide far.

Loggerhead turtles are very good swimmers.

Loggerhead turtle

How do turtles swim?
Turtles have webbed feet, which they use like frogman flippers to swim. Sea turtles use their two front feet together and steer with their hind flippers. Although they look ungainly on land, in the water turtles are graceful animals.

9

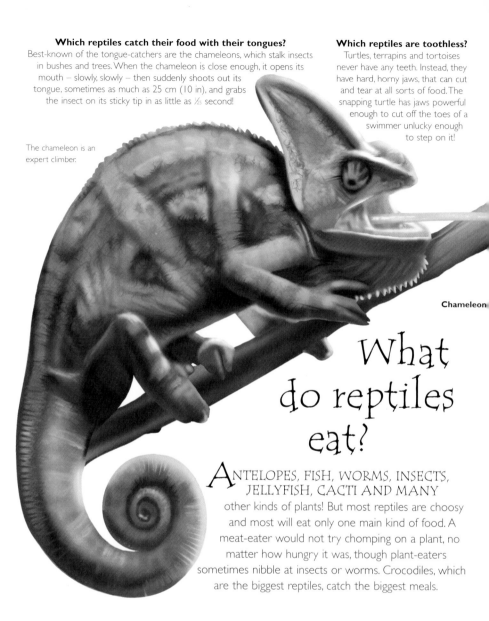

Which reptiles catch their food with their tongues?
Best-known of the tongue-catchers are the chameleons, which stalk insects in bushes and trees. When the chameleon is close enough, it opens its mouth – slowly, slowly – then suddenly shoots out its tongue, sometimes as much as 25 cm (10 in), and grabs the insect on its sticky tip in as little as ⅕ second!

Which reptiles are toothless?
Turtles, terrapins and tortoises never have any teeth. Instead, they have hard, horny jaws, that can cut and tear at all sorts of food. The snapping turtle has jaws powerful enough to cut off the toes of a swimmer unlucky enough to step on it!

The chameleon is an expert climber.

Chameleon

What do reptiles eat?

ANTELOPES, FISH, WORMS, INSECTS, JELLYFISH, CACTI AND MANY other kinds of plants! But most reptiles are choosy and most will eat only one main kind of food. A meat-eater would not try chomping on a plant, no matter how hungry it was, though plant-eaters sometimes nibble at insects or worms. Crocodiles, which are the biggest reptiles, catch the biggest meals.

How often do reptiles eat?
Reptiles that eat large meals don't need to eat very often. One that has just gorged itself on a huge meal may not eat again for several months. Very big snakes and crocodiles have been known to go for over two years between meals!

Do most reptiles eat big meals?
Big reptiles eat big meals for their size. A crocodile may scoff a buffalo or a young giraffe, but a little lizard is content with a few insects.

How do reptiles find their food?
Some use their eyes, first noticing the movements made by their prey before starting to stalk it. Others use their sense of smell, which in many cases is better than that of any bloodhound.

How does reptile poison work?

The venom that some reptiles produce works in two ways. Part of it paralyses the nervous system of the prey. The other part acts as a digestive juice to break down the prey's body, so venomous reptiles can digest their meals more quickly.

Why are some reptiles poisonous?

POISONOUS REPTILES USUALLY FEED ON ANIMALS THAT MOVE FASTER THAN they can, so they would probably get away if they were just bitten, but the venom (poison) stops them from escaping. Not all reptiles are poisonous. But two kinds of lizard and about a third of all known snakes have venomous bites.

Do reptiles pick up their food to eat it?

Most reptiles use their heads and teeth to catch their prey, but they don't hold it in their claws. Tortoises and some terrapins put their front feet on their food while they tear at it with their jaws, but they can't pick it up to make eating a meal easier.

Do reptiles need to drink?

All animals need water and reptiles are no exception. Some drink large quantities when water is available and are able to store it in a dry season. Giant snakes that may not eat for a long time still need to drink between meals.

Do reptiles chew their food?

No, they don't. Reptiles that feed on flesh generally swallow their meals whole, or in very large chunks. Plant-eating reptiles have teeth or jaws that cut their food up, but they don't grind it into small pieces like horses or rabbits do.

Which reptiles like eating jellyfish?

Almost all marine turtles eat some jellyfish, but the great leathery turtle feeds on little else. It seems strange that this armoured reptile, which may weigh up to 680 kg (1,500 lb) and be as long as a tall man, should eat only soft, jellylike creatures.

Gila monster

Galapagos tortoise

What reptiles are vegetarian?

The chief plant-eaters among the reptiles are the land tortoises and some lizards. Pet tortoises often eat favourite plants in your garden! The giant tortoises from the Galapagos Islands feed mainly on hard, prickly cacti. Some plant-eating lizards always go for yellow flowers. The strangest plant-eater of all is the marine iguana, which feeds on seaweeds.

Why do reptiles change colour?
Reptiles, particularly lizards, can change their colours for many reasons. They tend to be more intensely coloured In bright light, and paler in dull light. Often this helps to camouflage the animal. The lizard may also change colour when angry or frightened, as changes in colour can make it look bigger or fiercer. The most striking colour changes are in courtship displays, when male lizards confront mates or rivals.

How quickly can a reptile change colour?
Flash changes of colour take a fraction of a second. Pigment changes take longer – but not that long, as a chameleon can make a complete colour change in only two minutes! However, becoming paler in dim light may take hours or even weeks.

Can reptiles see in colour like we can?
Reptiles that are active in daylight can probably see much the same colours as we can. Lizards can distinguish red, orange, yellow, yellowish green, blue and violet. Giant tortoises can see orange, blue and green and some terrapins are very sensitive to reds. They may even be able to see infra-red, which is invisible to us.

Do reptiles change colour as they grow?
Brightly coloured reptiles such as lizards and snakes may change colour as they grow. This is usually because as they become bigger they begin to live in slightly different places and need to match different backgrounds. The dull browns and greys of turtles and crocodiles remain the same all their life.

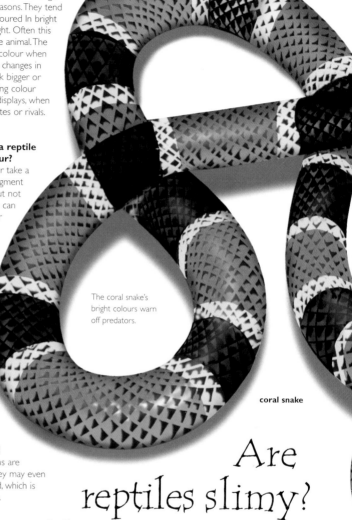

The coral snake's bright colours warn off predators.

coral snake

Are reptiles slimy?

No, REPTILES ARE NEVER SLIMY. IN SOME CASES THE SKIN IS ROUGH TO TOUCH, but many people are surprised at how beautifully silky the skin of a snake or a lizard can feel. The scales that cover most reptiles have very few glands, like our sweat glands, which is why the skin is dry. The scales help to protect the animal, and the thin skin between them is often folded. When a reptile like a snake eats a huge meal, its skin can bulge as the folds are stretched out.

How can you tell male and female reptiles apart?

Some male lizards are brightly coloured in the breeding season, which makes them attractive to females. (It also makes it easier for us to tell their sex.) The other differences between the sexes lie in shape, size and smell.

This anole lizard uses his brightly coloured throat fan to attract a mate.

Green anole lizard

Which reptiles wear armour?

THE BODIES OF TORTOISES, TERRAPINS AND TURTLES ARE ENCASED in bone that forms their protective shell. The shell is made even stronger by a cover of plates of horn. Crocodiles also wear armour, made of little bones called osteoderms, which are set in the skin. This armour protects them against most enemies.

Why are some reptiles bright red and black?

The venomous lizards and some small poisonous snakes called coral snakes are black and orange or red. This is called warning coloration, for it tells predators that animals with this colour are dangerous. Really large poisonous snakes are not brilliantly coloured, perhaps because they are not attacked by small predators.

Why do some snakes borrow dangerous colours?

A predator that has had a bad experience with a poisonous snake will probably avoid other snakes with a red and black warning coloration. So a few non-poisonous snakes are also red and black. They have evolved by tricking predators into thinking they are dangerous when they're not.

Which reptile has an invisible shadow?

Lichen bark geckos are little lizards that live in Madagascar. They are hard to see as they rest on the trunk of a tree, because they completely match the colour of their background. They also have a narrow flap of skin that runs round their body and drapes on to the tree. This hides the animal's shadow, which might be a give-away to hunters.

How do reptiles regulate their temperature?

They manage to keep at the best temperature for their needs by moving in and out of the sun and shade. As they bask in the sunshine they absorb the heat that they need for being active. Once they are active they create a little more heat. The leathery turtle, which is very active, is thought by some people to be partly warm-blooded, like a mammal.

How fast does a baby reptile grow?

IN THE EARLY DAYS OF LIFE MOST BABY REPTILES GROW QUITE QUICKLY.

Some alligators, which are about 20 cm (8 in) long at hatching, grow about 30 cm (12 in) a year for the first three years. After that they slow down, though they carry on growing for many more years.

Are reptiles good, caring parents?

Not usually! Most reptiles don't look after their families at all, so the babies have to fend for themselves. Baby reptiles are like small copies of their parents. Most are born from eggs laid by the mother. They hatch out of the egg fully formed and ready to go. They may be a different colour from the adults and often feed on different food for a while, but for a young reptile, independence is the name of the game.

When do male reptiles get really angry?

In the breeding season. Male reptiles may fight for territory and sometimes for mates. The most fearsome fighters are the big monitor lizards, which wrestle and tear at each other with their sharp claws. Some snakes twist round each other and sway in a battle – it looks as if they are dancing. The winner probably earns the right to the biggest female and the best place for egg-laying.

Which reptile lays most eggs?

Geckos usually lay only one or two eggs, but most reptiles produce more than this. Usually a big, old reptile lays more eggs than a small, young female. The biggest clutches of eggs are laid by green turtles, which normally produce over 100 – and sometimes as many as 200 – eggs!

How long does a baby reptile take to develop in the egg?

A long time – much longer than birds with eggs of a similar size. The baby tuatara takes the longest time of all reptiles to develop in its egg – up to 14 months! For many reptiles, the length of time in the egg may depend on the the temperature – the colder it is the more slowly they develop.

How does a baby reptile get out of its egg?

Before it hatches, a baby reptile grows a small, sharp bump on the end of its snout. This is called the "egg caruncle". When the little creature needs to break out of the egg, it twists its head from side to side and the caruncle breaks through the shell. Soon after this, the caruncle disappears.

Adders

These adders are "dancing" or fighting for a mate.

What is a reptile's egg like?

REPTILES' EGGS ARE WHITE OR DULL COLOURED, WITHOUT A POINTED end, like birds' eggs. Some have a hard shell, but many have a papery outer layer. They all have a yellow yolk, which is food for the embryo (developing young), plus a watery white. Some, but not all, have an air sac, which helps the young to breathe as they hatch out.

Crocodile young hatch from their eggs fully formed.

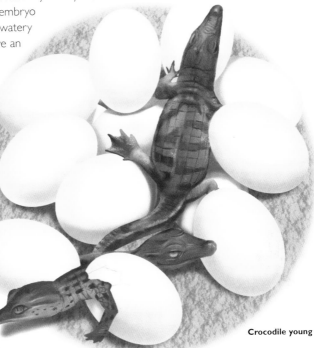

Crocodile young

Do any reptiles make good mothers?
Most reptile mothers don't look after their young. Crocodiles and alligators are the main exception. These scaly mothers guide their young, or sometimes carry them in their mouths, to the water. There they stay with them, to protect them from predators, often for several months.

Do reptile fathers ever help to bring up their families?
The male mugger, an Indian crocodile, sometimes crushes the eggs that are about to hatch very gently in his mouth, to help his babies into the world. With the female, he then escorts them down to the water. After this he may help to guard them, but does not teach them to care for themselves.

Which reptile babies don't hatch out of eggs?
All reptiles hatch out of eggs, but some hatch inside their mother's body. Some reptiles, including most of those that live in cold places, and the sea snakes, do not lay their eggs but hold them inside their bodies. Mostly these eggs have very thin shells and eventually the young break through and are born fully formed from their mother's body. She doesn't look after them beyond birth.

Are any baby reptiles born like mammals?
In some geckos and skinks the eggs that the mother holds inside her body are very small. She overcomes this by giving some nourishment to the growing young before they are born. This is almost like the way that baby mammals develop in the womb.

Plesiosaurs swimming

Plesiosaurs were very common sea creatures during the Age of Reptiles.

When did the first reptiles roam the Earth?

THE OLDEST KNOWN FOSSILS OF REPTILES DATE BACK ABOUT 280 MILLION years. They were small lizard-like creatures that lived in damp forests. Palaeontologists, who study fossils, tell us that they probably laid shelled eggs and hid from danger in tree stumps.

What was the Age of Reptiles?

The Age of Reptiles lasted from about 200 million years ago until about 65 million years ago. During this time all the main kinds of land animals and many of those that lived in the sea were reptiles. Most of them are now extinct.

Why are modern reptiles sometimes called 'living fossils' ?

All the reptiles alive today are very similar to those that lived in the distant past. If we could go back to the days of the dinosaurs, we would see crocodiles and turtles and some snakes and lizards. These "living fossils" can tell us a lot about prehistoric life.

What did the dinosaurs eat?

The dinosaurs are the best known prehistoric animals. *Tyrannosaurus*, which stood as tall as a house, was a flesh-eater that tore at its food with up to 60 teeth, each like a double edged saw. Not all dinosaurs were flesh eaters – many ate plants. Some chewed them well; others gulped them down and swallowed stones to help break them up in their stomachs.

Brachiosaurus was the tallest known dinosaur. With its long neck it would have been as tall as a three-storey house.

Brachiosaurus

How do dinosaurs get their names?

Names like *Tyrannosaurus*, which we use today, were given by the scientists who first studied the remains of the creature. Usually the name tells us something about the animal, or where it came from. *Tyrannosaurus* means terrifying lizard!

What colour were dinosaurs?

NO ONE KNOWS. IN A FEW CASES PIECES OF FOSSILISED SKIN have been found. Most look hard and warty. Very occasionally, there are marks that show where the living animal had stripes or colour changes. Like most modern reptiles, the dinosaurs were probably rather dull colours.

How can we tell what dinosaurs ate?

Teeth are always the clue to what an animal eats. Slicing daggers, like the teeth of *Tyrannosaurus*, could only belong to a flesh-eater, while a set of flat-topped grinding teeth like those of the duck-billed dinosaurs shows clearly that these animals fed on tough plant food.

Which was the first dinosaur to be discovered?

It is likely that ancient people sometimes found the bones of dinosaurs, but didn't know what they were. The first dinosaur to be discovered and recognised as a huge reptile was a flesh-eater called *Megalosaurus*.

Which was the first dinosaur to be given a name?

The first dinosaur to be given a name was not, strangely, the first one to be discovered. Some big teeth were found by a doctor's wife in Sussex, UK, in 1823. They turned out to belong to a big plant-eater that was called *Iguanodon* by the scientists who studied it.

Where is the best place to find dinosaur fossils?

In a museum! Lots have wonderful collections of fossil bones. But the best place to find them yourself – if you are very lucky – is in stream beds or by the seashore, where rocks of the right age may contain ancient remains.

**Alligator
snapping turtle**

The alligator
snapping turtle can
live to over 100 years old.

How does the snapping turtle fool its prey?

The Alligator Snapping Turtle Sits in the Water with its Mouth

open. It doesn't need to be very active, for on its tongue is a pink, worm-like growth which it waves gently in the current. Any fish stupid enough to nibble the "worm" is caught in the snapper's sharp jaws.

What's the difference between a tortoise and a terrapin?

Difficult to tell at first, because tortoises and terrapins are both slow-moving armoured reptiles. Tortoises live on dry land in many warm parts of the world. They usually have high-domed shells and feed mainly on plants. Terrapins live in fresh water. They have flattened shells, which make them more streamlined as they swim. They often have partly webbed feet and they feed on fish and other animals. Some terrapins are quite large, fierce predators.

So what is a turtle?

Some people use the word "turtle" to include tortoises and terrapins. But true turtles are big animals that live in the sea. Their shells are streamlined and they can't pull their heads inside for protection. Their feet are paddles covered in a mitten of skin, and they eat a mixture of sea plants and animals.

How many tortoises and terrapins are there?

There are 240 different kinds of tortoises, terrapins and turtles to be found in the world today. The scientific name for the whole group is the *Chelonia*. The biggest is the leatherback turtle, which may reach 1.8 m (13 feet) in length and weigh an astonishing 680 kg (1,500 lb). The smallest is the speckled tortoise, which is only about 10 cm (4 in) long when fully grown.

How is the shell joined to the tortoise?

A tortoise's armour is made of bone overlaid with horn. The bones are part of the skeleton, which have grown together to make a complete box. The backbones, ribs, hips and shoulders are all attached to this.

How do tortoises breathe?

Because their bodies are enclosed in a bony box, tortoises can't stretch their rib cage, and so they can't breathe like other animals. Instead they have special muscles that pull at the lungs, so that air is forced in and pushed out.

What drove many tortoises to extinction?

Human beings, unfortunately. The big members of the tortoise family are all very rare because they live on small islands. When sailors visited the islands in the past, before the days of refrigeration, they killed tortoises to get fresh meat. Many kinds of tortoise became extinct because of this.

Which Greek poet was killed by a tortoise?

The poet Aeschylus is supposed to have been killed by a tortoise in 455 BC. An eagle that had caught a tortoise thought the poet's bald head was a stone. It dropped its prey to crack it, but instead broke the poet's skull. Or so they say!

Why did the hawksbill turtle need protecting?

Tortoiseshell is the horny outer layer of the hawksbill turtle's shell. For many years hawksbills were hunted for their shells, which were made into all sorts of trinkets, boxes, fans and combs and sometimes used to decorate furniture. Now the hawksbill is endangered it's strictly protected, though in some parts of the world young hawksbills are reared specially to be killed for their shells.

How did a tortoise outrun a hare?

The ancient story of the hare and the tortoise tells how these two animals decided to have a race.

The hare was so confident that he would win, that he didn't bother to start until it was too late. The tortoise, plodding on, reached the finishing line first.

Why are some cats and butterflies called tortoiseshells?

They get their name because of their colours. The underside of the wings of the butterfly and the coat of the cat are blotched with black, brown and gold. These are the colours of tortoiseshell taken from the hawksbill turtles' shell.

Which creature lives in a box?

The box turtle is a small tortoise with a hinged shell. When it is alarmed it pulls in its head and feet and shuts the lid, so it is totally enclosed in its shell. A hunter like a fox is fooled by the bony box.

Can tortoises climb trees?

THE CHINESE BIG-HEADED TURTLE HAS LONG claws and a long tail. This cumbersome creature is more agile than it looks. When it's out of water, it sometimes scrambles up trees for safety. All its relatives stay firmly on the ground!

Chinese big-headed turtle

Despite its heavy shell, the big-headed turtle can scramble up trees using its long claws to grip and its tail to balance.

19

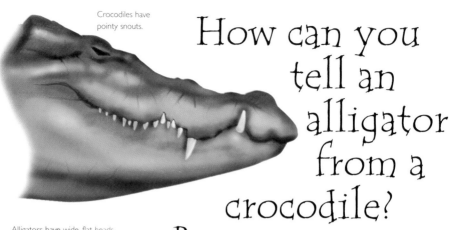

Crocodiles have pointy snouts.

How can you tell an alligator from a crocodile?

Alligators have wide, flat heads and rounded noses.

By ITS SMILE! ALLIGATORS AND THEIR RELATIVES THE CAIMANS ARE VERY similar to crocodiles and their cousin the gharial. They are all water-living hunters with long jaws crammed with sharp pointed teeth. The easiest way to tell one from the other is that when an alligator has its mouth closed, you can't see any of its lower teeth. A crocodile shows a big tooth sticking up at either side of its mouth.

Like alligators, caimans have wide, flat heads and rounded noses.

Which mother carries its babies in its fearsome mouth?
Mother crocodiles help their young by breaking away the hard cap of soil over the nest, and digging down to the eggs. They sometimes break the eggs gently in their mouths to free the babies, which are only about 20 cm (8 in) long. When the family is complete, the mother either leads them down to the water, or carries them – carefully! – in her mouth. For the first months of their life, she protects them by driving away enemies such as storks or other crocodiles.

What does a baby crocodile eat?
After it has finished eating the yolk from its egg, the baby crocodile starts to catch insects. These are its most important prey until it is about two years old.

Gharials have long, thin snouts that they use for fishing.

Why is the crocodile in danger?
Some types of crocodile have become very rare because people have destroyed their habitat. Many other types have been hunted to the brink of extinction. Only now that crocodiles are disappearing have people discovered their importance to the environment.

What are crocodile tears?
Crocodile tears are not real tears of sadness. So someone crying crocodile tears is insincere. This idea came from a sea captain called John Hawkins. He said that a crocodile would cry, then eat any creature stupid enough to be sorry for it.

Do crocodiles use birds as toothbrushes?
In a way, yes! The Nile crocodile often rests with its mouth open. Birds venture into its open jaws to pick at bits of meat stuck between the teeth, and perhaps feed on parasites lurking there as well. The birds have to leap out of the way if the crocodile suddenly snaps shut its jaws. By taking flight, they can also warn the crocodile of approaching danger.

Why don't crocodiles need sunshades?
The heavy skin of a crocodile is protected by scales. In some place these are like thick toenails, in others they have become bone. The bony scales are called osteoderms. Osteoderms act as armour against attack, and also against overheating when the crocodile is basking in the sun.

Do crocodiles like getting water up their noses?
No. They prefer calm water to swim in. To swim, a crocodile holds its front feet close to its body and forges forwards, using its powerful tail like a paddle. If the water is choppy, the crocodile has to raise its head to stop the water getting up its nose.

Where are crocodiles farmed?
In many parts of the world where crocodiles have become very rare, people are now breeding them in in crocodile farms. Some are released into the wild but most are killed and used for leather and for meat.

Which animal has 45 sets of teeth before it is fully grown?
Even if it could, a crocodile never has any need to wear false teeth. As the animal grows and its teeth wear down, they are replaced by sharp new ones growing in its jaws. By the time it is a young adult, a Nile crocodile will probably have used up 45 sets of teeth!

How do baby crocodiles call their mum?
When they are ready to hatch, baby crocodiles croak to their mother from inside the egg. Then she knows it's time to help them hatch. In the water she warns them of danger by twitching her body. The babies feel the water swirling and cluster round her for safety.

When do kids walk like crocodiles?
When they walk two by two. A line of schoolchildren walking in pairs is called a crocodile. This is probably because they don't walk in a dead straight line, but curve a little from side to side, like a crocodile's long body as it swims.

The spur-winged plover picks pieces of meat from between the crocodile's teeth.

Basking crocodile

Which is the biggest living crocodile?

The saltwater crocodile. The largest one recorded so far is over 7 m (23 feet) long. Others are said to have grown even bigger – in some cases to over 9 m (29 feet) long – though no accurate records of these have been kept.

Why should you avoid being bitten by a beaded lizard?

You can tell a beaded lizard because its scales make it look as though it has been sprinkled all over with beads. But the great difference between beaded lizards and other lizards is that they have a poisonous bite. They eat mainly small helpless creatures, and use the bite for self-defence.

Which lizard has eaten people?

The biggest of all lizards is called the Komodo dragon. This fearsome creature measures up to 3 m (10 feet) long and weighs over 150 kg (330 lb). It normally feeds on carrion (animals it finds already dead), but it has been known to kill and eat humans!

What lizard flies?

Lizards cannot fly like birds, but some forest dwellers can glide for about 20 m (65 feet) between trees. As they leap from a branch they spread a flap of skin supported by ribs.

Which lizards have the biggest stomachs?

American horned lizards and the Australian moloch lizard feed on nothing but ants. A single meal may consist of 2,500 ants! Their stomachs have to be much larger than average so they can eat such big meals, and may be up to 13% of their total bulk.

What is a sandfish?

A sandfish is not a fish at all, but a smooth, shiny-skinned lizard called a skink, that lives in sand dunes. Its legs are tiny, so to get about in its sandy home it wriggles its way along with side-to-side movements, like a snake.

What creature shoots blood from its eyes?

If a horned lizard is attacked, it can increase the blood pressure in veins in its eye sockets until they burst. Blood squirts out in a thin stream, travelling up to 122 cm (48 in) and splattering the attacker. Predators that get the lizard's blood in their eyes or mouth think it is poisonous and leave the lizard alone.

Where do lizards live?

There are at least 2,500 different kinds of lizards. Except for Antarctica and some very small islands, they live in almost every country in the world. Most of them are found in warm places, but a few live as far north as the Arctic Circle.

Is it true that some lizards have no legs?

YES, QUITE A LOT OF LIZARDS ARE LEGLESS – THEY WRIGGLE ALONG LIKE SNAKES.
Scientists think that the ancestors of these lizards were burrowing creatures, which wriggled their way through the soil. Their legs were not used for this activity, so gradually grew smaller and eventually disappeared altogether.

The Californian legless lizard looks more like a snake than a lizard.

Californian legless lizard

How does a frilled lizard scare its enemies?

Tʜᴇ ꜰʀɪʟʟᴇᴅ ʟɪᴢᴀʀᴅ ᴛᴜʀɴꜱ ᴏɴ ɪᴛꜱ ᴇɴᴇᴍɪᴇꜱ, ᴏᴘᴇɴꜱ its mouth wide and at the same time spreads a big ruff of brightly coloured skin round its neck. This makes it look much larger and fiercer than it really is. Quite often the bluff works and the lizard escapes with its life.

Frilled lizard

Is it true that lizards never stop growing?

Like all reptiles, lizards grow fast when they are young. After they are big enough to mate, they grow more slowly, but it is likely that they don't ever stop growing completely. Tiny lizards are probably short-lived, but the big ones are almost all very old.

What creature can grow two tails?

A lizard's tail may break if bitten by an attacker. At first the tail wriggles all on its own, and the predator is distracted by the twitching tail while the lizard escapes.

What creature blows itself up like a balloon?

Chuckwallas live in North American deserts. If one is attacked it dives into a crevice in the rocks and swallows air, so its body is blown up like a balloon. However hard the predator tries to dislodge it, it is unlikely to succeed, for the chuckwalla is stuck in its crevice and can't be budged.

If its vivid ruff doesn't scare off enemies, the frilled lizard will either run away or run towards its enemies, hissing.

Horned lizards are decreasing in number, though no one is really sure why.

Horned lizard

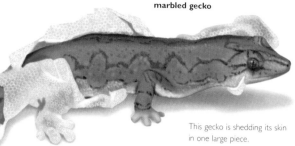
marbled gecko

This gecko is shedding its skin in one large piece.

When is a lizard like a hedgehog?
When threatened by a larger enemy, the spiny lizard of South Africa rolls itself up and holds its tail in its mouth. The predator is faced with a prickly ball, which it usually leaves well alone.

How does a lizard shed its skin?

Which lizard can move its eyes independently?
The chameleon! Its eyes are partly surrounded by skin, and look as if they are in little turrets. Each eye can be swivelled independently, so a chameleon can always see what is going on around it.

LIKE US, LIZARDS NEED TO SHED THEIR SKIN. BUT WHILE WE LOSE OUR SKIN ALL THE time in minute flakes, lizards shed theirs from time to time in large pieces. Sometimes a lizard will pull a piece of skin off with its teeth, and eat it. Underneath is a bright new skin.

When does a lizard look like a snake?
Several kinds of lizard are left alone by their enemies because they look like poisonous snakes. They have similar colouring and move their heads in a snake-like way. One lizard that lives in Pakistan has a tail that looks like a viper, which it waves to warn off enemies. Some lizards escape from their enemies because when they stand still they look like plants!

Why do lizards pretend to be beetles?
One little lizard that lives in the Kalahari Desert has a tail coloured like desert sand. The rest of its body is black and white, so while the tail disappears into the background, the body looks like a horrid-tasting desert beetle. Predators that have learnt that the beetle is nasty avoid the lizard. As it grows too big to be mistaken for a beetle, the lizard loses its black and white colouring and becomes camouflaged against its desert background.

Where can you see lizards in the sky?
Look up into the sky on a summer night in the northern hemisphere and you can see the constellation of Draco, the dragon or lizard, with its tail curling round the Little Bear. In the southern hemisphere a constellation called the Chameleon has its long tongue pointing towards a smaller star group called the Fly.

Where does a lizard hold the purse strings?

In the past, the Japanese carried purses fastened by toggles called netsuke. These were often carved in the shape of lizards twined around each other.

Lizards can move much faster on hind legs than they can on all fours.

Why do some lizards have very fat tails?

Lizards that live on the edge of deserts, where there is rainfall and food for part of the year only, eat as much as they can in times of plenty. They store food as fat in their bodies, usually round the tail, which grows very big and fat. When there is no food, the tail slims down again as the fat is used up to give the lizard energy.

Do lizards eat seaweed?

The only seaweed-eating lizard is the marine iguana from the Galapagos Islands. It lives on the seashore and dives into the water to feed on weeds that grow on rocks. The sea off the Galapagos is cooled by the Humboldt Current, but the iguana can drop its heart rate so it does not slow down in the cold, as other reptiles do. The marine iguana also has special glands that get rid of salt from the water.

Can lizards walk on water?

No! But the basilisk lizards of South America can run over water for a few seconds at their top speed of about 8 kph (5 mph). The water surface film does not support them for long. But by the time they sink they have usually escaped the enemy that was chasing them into the water.

Why are some lizards black?

You can often find black lizards in high mountains where the sunlight is bright but the air is cold. Their black skins allow them to warm up better than if they had a pale skin. In just one hour in the sun, the lava lizard of the Peruvian Andes mountains can raise its temperature to 33°C — when the temperature of the air around it is only 1.5°C.

Why do lizards stand on tip-toe?

SOME DESERT-LIVING LIZARDS STAND ON TIP-TOE BECAUSE THE GROUND HAS got too hot. Others stand on their hind legs so they can see further. Still others run on their hind legs so they don't waste energy wriggling from side to side.

Gould's monster

How many kinds of snake are there?
There are around 2,500 different kinds of snake known in the world today. Most live in warm countries, though you are not likely to see them, since they are generally shy creatures.

Which is the smallest snake?
The smallest snakes are the blind or thread snakes. They are rarely spotted, as they burrow underground. Some are only 15 cm (6 in) long when fully grown. They normally feed on ants and termites, which they hunt by smell.

Can snakes shut their eyes?
A snake has no eyelids, so it can't shut its eyes, even when it's asleep. As it moves about, its eyes are protected by a transparent scale called a brille. Many people think that snakes have an evil stare, but this is simply because they can't blink.

Can snakes hear through their jaws?
Snakes have no eardrums, so they can hardly hear any airborne sounds. But they do have an ear bone that connects with the lower jaw, so they can sense vibrations through their jaw from the ground or water. Like other animals, they have an inner ear which is used for balance.

The fork in the snake's tongue is very sensitive.

Why do snakes have forked tongues?

So they can 'taste' their way

about the world. As the tongue flickers out of the snake's mouth, it picks up tiny particles of scent left by other animals. Inside the snake's mouth is a pit lined with cells that are very sensitive to smells. The tongue flickers in the air or on to the ground, then is pushed into the pit to test for smells that might lead to food. The deep fork means that the snake can sample a wider track than it could with a simple, undivided tongue.

Why do snakes swallow their food whole?
Snakes' teeth are sharply pointed, good for holding food, but no use for cutting it up or chewing it. So when a snake has caught a meal, it has to swallow it in one piece. It may have to unhitch its jaws so that a really big meal can go down. You can tell when a snake has just eaten well because of the bulge in its body.

Do snakes ever have legs?
No snake has legs, but a few kinds have tiny claws towards their rear end. These, and some small bones inside the body, are the only remains of the legs that their ancestors once had.

Which is the biggest snake?

THE LONGEST OF ALL SNAKES IS THE RETICULATED PYTHON FROM Indonesia. It is often longer than 6 m (19 feet), with some running to over 10 m (32 feet). The heaviest snake is the anaconda, which is usually shorter than the python, but much stouter. An anaconda measuring only 5.2 m (17 feet) weighs as much as a python of 7.3 m (24 feet).

The golden tree snake is one of several flying snakes.

How does a flying snake fly?
No snake can fly like a bird, but the golden tree snake comes nearest to it. As it launches itself from a branch, it pulls in its belly, so it is concave, like a long wing, and shaped like this it can glide for several metres.

Golden tree snake

Are snakes aggressive?
Most snakes are peaceable animals, and hurry away from trouble if they can. Humans are not the natural prey of snakes, so most are aggressive towards us only if they are cornered. Most are non-poisonous, but even so, it's best to leave them alone.

What is a snakestone?
A snakestone is the name that used to be given to fossils of ammonites, because their curled shells reminded people of snakes. You can sometimes see these fossils in antique shops, with snakes' heads carved on to them.

What is a constrictor?
A constrictor means a squeezer – it's a snake that squeezes its prey to death. It does this by throwing a loop of its body round the prey. It then squeezes so hard that the prey is soon suffocated, and the snake can swallow its meal.

By stretching its mouth, the boa constrictor can swallow its prey whole.

Boa constrictor

Can snakes spit their venom?

SPITTING COBRAS HAVE A TINY HOLE IN THEIR POISON FANGS THROUGH

which they can spit their venom. The poison can be spat up to 2 m (6 feet) with a spread of over 0.5 m (19 in). Snakes aim for their enemies' eyes, where the venom causes severe pain and at least temporary blindness.

Which Greek god has snakes around his staff?

Hermes, messenger to the gods, is often carrying a staff with two snakes twined round it. Greek mythology says that these were originally two white ribbons. Then Hades, who ruled over the kingdom of the dead, gave Hermes the job of laying his staff on the eyes of the dying, and turned the ribbons into snakes.

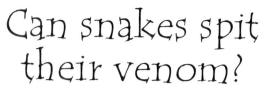

Black spitting cobra

Why haven't snakes got legs?

The early ancestors of snakes did have legs, and they could walk about like other animals. Most scientists think that some of these snakes took to burrowing in the ground, where legs were not much use, so they lost them. Since then some snakes have returned to the surface, but their legs have gone for good.

What is a front-fanged snake?

It's a snake with a poisonous bite. The poison is made in glands high up at the back of the jaw, then channelled to the fangs (hollow teeth) in the front of the mouth. When the snake bites, poison flows down the fangs straight into the wound.

How do you milk a snake?

Milking a snake means taking venom from it. This is a job for an expert, who holds the snake so that its mouth is open and its fangs are in a small jar. The snake is usually fairly cross at this treatment and bites at the jar, so that venom flows into it from its fangs. The venom is used to make medicines for blood-clotting disorders, as well as antidotes (cures) for people who have been bitten by snakes.

Which is the most dangerous snake?

The snake with the deadliest poison is the olive sea snake, but like all snakes, it is shy and rarely spotted. Far more dangerous are land-living species, such as cobras and rattlesnakes. The eastern diamondback rattlesnake is said to be the most dangerous snake in North America. In fact all venomous snakes can be dangerous. People should not try to kill them, for they have their own place in the ecosystem in which they live.

What was a snake doing in the Garden of Eden?

The snake in the Garden of Eden is supposed to have tempted Eve, the first woman in the Old Testament creation story, to take the fruit of the tree of knowledge – and this has led to all our troubles ever since!

How do snake charmers charm snakes?

Snake charmers in India keep cobras or other very poisonous snakes in a sack. To entertain people, they play the flute, and the snake writhes out of the sack and dances to the music. But, since the snake has no ears it can't actually hear the music! In fact it weaves its head about as it watches the movements of the flute or feels the vibration of the charmer's tapping feet.

Cobras are one of only four types of poisonous snakes.

Rattlesnake

Rattlesnakes are dangerous to humans only if disturbed.

How does a rattlesnake rattle?

A RATTLESNAKE'S RATTLE IS MADE OF INTERLOCKING PIECES OF HARD material like toenails, which tap against each other when the end of the tail is twitched. The rattle grows longer each time the snake sheds its skin, so an old rattlesnake will have a bigger rattle than a young one. The rattle is used to warn off large animals.

What is "a snake in the grass"?

The phrase "a snake in the grass" means a hidden enemy. It was first used in Roman times, when people went barefoot or wore open sandals, and were sometimes in danger of stepping on venomous snakes.

How do some snakes play possum?

When they are caught, or badly frightened, some snakes pretend to be dead. A snake playing possum rolls limply on to its back, dislocates its jaws, and hangs its tongue out of its mouth. But the snake is not dead, and after a few minutes of acting, it will turn over and slip quickly away.

How many people do reptiles kill every year?
Poisonous snakes bite large numbers of people every year, though there are no reliable figures to say how many attacks are fatal. Modern treatment means that far more people survive snakebites than used to be the case. Saltwater crocodiles and Nile crocodiles attack and probably kill up to 3,000 people a year.

Which animal in Britain has killed most people?
The adder is the biggest poisonous animal in Britain, but it has not caused the most human deaths. Guess which creature has – the honey bee! Some people are allergic to bee stings and have died from them.

How many reptiles do people kill every year?
It's not possible to say, but we are more dangerous to reptiles than they are to us! Most of the large tortoises that used to inhabit remote islands have been hunted to extinction, and countless smaller reptiles have been lost because of habitat destruction. Today most marine turtles and most crocodiles are so rare that they are nearly extinct. A number of lizards and snakes are in the same plight.

Which reptiles are valued for their skin?
Many reptiles have been hunted to the brink of extinction for their beautiful skins. The skins of large lizards and snakes are especially valuable, as is the skin of the underside of the crocodile. Some hunters sell the skin of marine turtles' flippers, pretending that it's something more valuable.

Do reptiles make good pets?

Reptiles are not like other pets; they must have warmth and the right food and housing if they are to thrive. They may need vitamin supplements and ultra-violet light to keep them healthy. Many people don't realise that reptiles are hard to look after, need a lot of attention and money spent on them and may soon grow very large and become hard to manage.

What is the worst time of year to meet an adder?
Early in the spring is the most dangerous time to meet poisonous snakes in cool parts of the world. In spring snakes aren't very quick to warm up and you could step on one before it has the chance to get away. Most snakebites occur at this time.

Are reptiles welcome in the garden?

Yes – apart from large poisonous snakes! Few reptiles that wander into your garden are likely to eat cherished plants. Their food generally consists of pest species such as mice and large insects. In Northern Europe, a legless lizard called a slow worm feeds largely on small slugs – creatures that most gardeners are pleased to be rid of.

Loggerhead turtles

Loggerhead turtles arrive on a breeding beach.

What help is on hand for sea turtles?

Endangered sea turtles are being helped by people who organise sanctuaries on their breeding beaches where the young can hatch in safety. Sometimes the young are kept in the sanctuary until they are large enough to stand a good chance of survival in the ocean.

What are herpetologists?

People who study reptiles. Herpetologist comes from a Greek word meaning creeping, that was used to describe reptiles. There are no commonly used terms for specialists who study, for instance, only lizards or turtles.

What is lucky in China but evil in the West?

Dragons! These mythical beasts are scaly, sharp-toothed and long-tailed. They have leathery wings, and some can breathe fire. In Western folklore they are evil, destroying people and their crops. In China they are a force for good, warding off evil spirits.

In China the dragon is seen as a sign of good.

Which snakes once won a battle for humans?

Hannibal, the Carthaginian general, ordered jars of live snakes to be thrown aboard the ships of his enemy. His terrified foes soon gave in.

Do people ever eat reptiles?

A FEW REPTILES EAT PEOPLE, BUT THIS IS NOTHING TO THE AMOUNT OF alligator meat, snake meat and turtle meat eaten by humans. In some parts of the world, reptiles are farmed for their meat. Reptile meat is good, for it is tasty and has very little fat.

Index